PRAISE FOR *IT'S IN THE TOOLBOX*

Prior to his ministry, Jesus was trained by his father Joseph to work with his hands, to work with wood and stone. Jesus' father would have taught him to use the right tool for the right job. Jesus knew the importance of tools. In this brief, but important small group men's study, Greg May connects the tools of the laborer with the insights of what is needed for men to grow in their relationship to one another in Christian fellowship as well as deepening their relationship with Jesus Christ. The men who choose to venture into this "toolbox" of spiritual formation will undoubtedly find important resources that will strengthen their faith.

Dr. Allan R. Bevere
Pastor First United Methodist Church
Cambridge, OH

It's In The Toolbox is a must have tool or resource for leaders of small groups or Sunday School classes. Greg May, a personal friend of mine, has been there, done that, and has several Tee shirts to prove it. He is truly a MAN of God, a loving father and a devoted husband who has a way with words that can be easily understood by anyone. Each lesson in this book was written so that the average "Joe" could identify with the examples used and the scriptures cited were easy to read and comprehend. The thought provoking discussion questions following each lesson should definitely lead to interesting and meaningful discussions with any "Manly" group. If you have the responsibility to be a group leader or facilitator, this book will be a great asset for you. It is my sincere belief that most men will be able to identify with each lesson and that a lot of thought provoking discussions will ensue by using this resource. I think many men will benefit from using this book and will enjoy a closer relationship with God by using it.

Terrell D. Bridges, Lt.Col, USA, Ret.

How wonderful! *It's in the Toolbox* was fun, easy to read and kept my interest (and I'm a girl). And the analogies were spot-on great! I could picture so many tool scenes in my head, yet Greg tied it all in with Scripture so well. It's going to be a huge hit with men's Bible study groups. This is practical, hands-on Christianity!

Kimberly Gordon
author *It's in the Bag, Please Love Me*

I must confess something to you. I have sinned. It is a sin I have struggled with for twenty years of my Christian life. I don't like Christian books. Why? It seems like every Christian fiction book I read ends up perfectly, all wrapped up neatly with a big red bow, with everyone getting saved or healed … and it seems like every devotional book is a mini-sermonette to enrich my time with my morning coffee. So, there it is … one of my great sins. I just want something "real." I want to feel like the author has as many struggles as me. I want someone who gets mad about dumb things, wakes up grumpy sometimes, grieves when things break their heart, and still manages to keep their ears and heart open to hear from God. That's what I continually find in Greg's writing. A real person who struggles with real things, who doesn't always say the right things, who gets snippy with their spouse and struggles to be the best parent they can. I like his writing for what it continually says to me … there's hope for you, too.

Erin McClellan, Youth Director
Pensacola, FL

It's
in the
Toolbox

Greg May

Energion Publications
energionpubs.com
2013

Cover Design: Nick May
Cover Image: Copyright © Olivierl | Dreamstime.com.
Used by permission

ISBN10: 1-938434-71-4
ISBN13: 978-1-938434-71-6
Library of Congress Control Number: 2013944162

Energion Publications
P. O. Box 841
Gonzalez, FL 32560

850-525-3916
energionpubs.com
pubs@energion.com

TABLE OF CONTENTS

This study is dedicated to the men who were the "testing ground" for this kind of gathering; where men can build trusting, Godly relationships with one another. Men who courageously meet the challenges of every day life and are willing to meet their challenges head-on, like men! They are genuine Warriors, sometimes wounded in the daily battle, yet are able to persevere by the power of God and with the help of their Brothers in Arms! They are good, Godly, mighty men in the Kingdom and they are lethal to the darkness of the enemy!

Thanks especially to Preston, Dimitrius, Jeff, Alan, Bo, and Tony.

As Iron Sharpens Iron ...

God has specifically designed us for relationships, to Him and to others. It is my prayer that this Bible study will help facilitate that in the lives of men.

It is not written just to give information, but to apply in a practical way the things God may show us in our daily life as growing men of God.

It is designed to be experienced in a small group setting. I would say 6-8 men max, committed to meeting maybe once a week for a few unrushed hours on each topic. This would allow time for a good amount of sharing and discussion.

The building of relationships filled with love, trust, prayer for each other and support will come as your group shares their life stories with one another. The discussion questions at the end of each topic will help guide a discussion. God will take it from there. Trust me, the more open, honest and caring your group is with each other the more you will see God move in your lives. He just needs your hearts to be open to Him!

As iron sharpens iron, so one man sharpens another (Proverbs 27:17).

Greg

1

Jesus Christ: Tough Guy, Man's Man

I think Jesus is and has often been viewed wrongly as a man, especially by men. When we see old movies, some music videos, Easter plays at church with the appearance of Jesus as a victim and Christmas as a helpless baby, it contributes to a world view of Jesus "the man" as soft and even wimpy. We continue to hear of His love and mercy as we read the Bible or listen to a preacher and some (men especially) scoff at the notion of outward expressions of love and caring for others. What a load of crap!

First let me say that His birth, death, resurrection, His compassion, love and mercy are all central to our faith in Him as believers. However, in this case, I am addressing the not so uncommon view, by mostly men, of Jesus the man as a soft, wimpy pushover.

Jesus was a carpenter. I have been a carpenter, a fisherman and a soldier and nothing is soft or wimpy in those occupations! I have worked on construction sites where carpenters endured extremes in weather and continual hard labor, and we had power tools. My grandfather was a carpenter and he thought he had it made when he got a circular saw! Do you think it was easier in Jesus' day?

Have you seen the various fishing shows on television where men fish for a living? Does that look like easy money? That was even harder back in Jesus' days on this earth! That's the kind of guys Jesus was around. He chose "real men" to be His disciples!

Not enough. How about Simon the Zealot? A rebel with a cause and I'll bet he would have fought the Romans to his death! He was one of Jesus' buds too!

Do you think it wimpy to go around the country openly preaching against the very people who want to kill you? How about willingly dying for those you care about? I don't think so. I think that's at the top of the courage scale!

How about the crucifixion? Check that out in Matthew 27 and John 19. Not for the faint of heart!

Do you fancy yourself a "real man"? Then how about following in the footsteps of a genuine "Tough Guy"?

Jesus Christ! Tough guy! Carpenter. Friend of fishermen and righteous rebels! Son of God! Loving and merciful Savior too!

GROUP DISCUSSION

1. What is your honest opinion of what a real man should be?

2. How do you honestly view Jesus, the man?

3. Wasn't Jesus strong, courageous and willing to sacrifice Himself for others? Didn't His closest followers include real men? Can't we be real men and follow Jesus too?

4. Jesus wants real men to be His followers! Pray that God will show you how to become a *real* man of God!

2

RECALCULATING (THE GPS)

While out on my route, I often have people stopping me to ask for directions. Some of you are probably thinking: "Tell 'em to get a GPS already! Man has figured out how to get anywhere!" Yet even with a GPS, we often find ourselves "recalculating."

This happened the other day as a lady stopped me to ask how to get to the airport. I'm getting this question a lot lately because the new airport is located several miles to the north of the old airport's location. It seems that many folks have not updated their GPS to guide them to the new airport.

Being from out of town, she had no clue how to get there. She couldn't even get her phone app to show her a map. Even with a map, you have to know the point at which you want to arrive.

The same holds true in the Kingdom. If we want to get to the Father God in Heaven, we have to know the way to His place. So many, while seeking God, are lost, turning aimlessly down one road after another, following some "Man's GPS."

There is a map, the Word of God. It has always been there and the route to Him remains the same. It never has been and never will need to be updated or recalculated! If someone who is lost reads and follows it, they will find their way to God's place. Man's GPS will not get them there!

There are also those who know how to get to His place because they know Him. Just like me telling the lost lady how to get to the airport, those that know God should be ready, willing and able to show those that are lost how to get to Him.

And just like there is only one road into our local airport, there is only one way to the Father!

Jesus said: "I am the way and the truth and the life. No one comes to the Father except through me." (John 14:6)

For the lost, not knowing how to get to God is going to be Hell! So I ask: "Why is it that so many are lost, when so many know the Way?"

GROUP DISCUSSION

1. Has your GPS ever steered you wrong? How? How far did you go out of the way before you stopped and asked directions, guys? Tell the truth! (At this point, you can ask any women who happen to be in the room to leave, so that you will not have to forfeit your man-card!)

2. Are you searching for God? Are you searching for His will? Check His map (The Bible), it tells of the Way to Him and His will for your life.

> *For God so loved the world that he gave his one and only Son, that whoever believes in him shall not perish but have eternal life. For God did not send his Son into the world to condemn the world, but to save the world through him.* (John 3:16-17)

> *Therefore, I urge you, brothers and sisters, in view of God's mercy, to offer your bodies as a living sacrifice, holy and pleasing to God—this is your true and proper worship. Do not conform to the pattern of this world, but be transformed by the renewing of your mind. Then you will be able to test and approve what God's will is—his good, pleasing and perfect will.* (Romans 12:1-2)

3. Pray that God will show you those who are seeking Jesus, the Way to Him.

3

Our Great Design

I am a capable carpenter, shade tree mechanic and all around decent handyman. I know the difference it makes to have the right tools designed for the job. Simply put, a wrench makes a lousy hammer, a hatchet makes a lousy saw and a screwdriver makes a lousy chisel. You know you've done it! Attempting to use tools for jobs other than what they are designed for is certain to bring on the stress of not reaching the "destiny" of a completed job, not to mention the satisfaction and joy of completion.

I believe much stress in our lives is brought on when we are not doing what we were designed to do. I'm not talking about vocation (this job or that job), but what we were all designed by our Creator to do: We were all designed for relationships, every one of us! A relationship to God and a relationship to other people.

> *One of the teachers of the law came and heard them debating. Noticing that Jesus had given them a good answer, he asked him, "Of all the commandments, which is the most important?"*
>
> *"The most important one," answered Jesus, "is this: 'Hear, O Israel: The Lord our God, the Lord is one. Love the Lord your God with all your heart and with all your soul and with all your mind and with all your strength.' The second is this: 'Love your neighbor as yourself.' There is no commandment greater than these."*
>
> *"Well said, teacher," the man replied. "You are right in saying that God is one and there is no other but him. To love him with all your heart, with all your understanding and with all your strength, and to love your neighbor as yourself is more important than all burnt offerings and sacrifices."* (Mark 12:28-33)

He put in us the desire to be loved and to want to give our love to others. If and when we spend our time and talents (our design) on other things because we mistakenly see them as more important, we will feel a misuse (stress or an internal lack) way down in our being. We know deep inside when we are being used other than for that which we were designed.

What's going to matter a hundred years from now? Our relationships, not how much stuff we accumulated! Our relationship to God will have eternal consequences. Our relationships to those we outrun to Heaven will mold them in some way or another. The legacy, memories and principles (not the stuff) we leave with them will affect their lives now and forever.

I have furniture my grandfather made that I consider priceless. I have pictures, trinkets, and all sorts of things that came from relatives and friends gone before me. These items remind me of them and I cherish this stuff. Yet I have to say I would trade any and all of it for five minutes with them right now, just to thank them for the time they spent with me.

GROUP DISCUSSION

1. What tools have you ever used for a job other than for one which they were designed? How did that work out for you? (Yeah, I'm smiling!)

2. Who has influenced your life greatly by spending their time with you, talking to you, and putting your wants and needs ahead of their own?

3. To whom are you, or can you, be a help and influence to?

4. What relationships do you have that are most important to you? Do you need to reassess and reprioritize them?

5. Ask God to guide you in keeping the priority of your relationships based on His two Greatest Commandments.

4

QUICK, EASY, ETERNAL

I like fixing things up, for instance remodeling a room in my house. I'm currently building a ramp on our deck. I'm enjoying this project. Yet I don't particularly like fixing broken stuff. For example, my truck engine stalls out and the brakes need work. I'm not looking forward to that job! I don't mind how long a project like painting or adding to the deck might take, but when something is broke, I want a quick and easy fix.

The other night our oven stopped working. I don't know about you, but for this southern boy, a broken oven is a priority-one emergency! Friends who have seen me eat know I am serious here! Anyway, I wanted a quick and easy fix. After determining that the heating element was shot (it was broken to pieces), I priced out the part. Twenty bucks and a few days delivery off the Internet *or* thirty-five dollars from the local appliance parts place to have it now. I headed for the parts store.

It was a bit pricey, but within fifteen minutes of opening the oven to fix it, the heat was on! It was quick and easy! I popped out two screws, unplugged the two connectors, hooked up the new element, screwed it back in and it was as good as new! There you go, my favorite kind of fix-it, quick and easy. Last night's chocolate chip cookies were awesome!

Sin will corrode our hearts, just like heat over the years burns out an oven's heating element. The repair of our hearts can be even quicker and easier than me fixing my oven. If your heart is corroded, broken and just doesn't get warm anymore, maybe sin has broken it to pieces. The Repairman to call is Jesus. Just ask Him to replace (forgive your sins) that worn, broken element inside with a new one. It's quick and easy, for us. Yet it was not so quick and easy for Him, and it was really pricey. It cost Him everything. Yet He gives it to us for free!

Oh yeah, His repair comes with an "Eternal Life Time Warranty!"

For the wages of sin is death, but the gift of God is eternal life in Christ Jesus our Lord. (Romans 6:23)

GROUP DISCUSSION

1. What have you had to repair lately? Was it quick and easy?

2. Why do we want quick and easy?

3. Are you experiencing any "corrosion on your burner"?

4. Ask God to show you any areas that sin may be corroding your life? If so, seek Him out for repairs!

If we confess our sins, he is faithful and just and will forgive us our sins and purify us from all unrighteousness. (1 John 1:9)

5

The Circular Saw

I remember going to my grandfather's house from the time I was a small boy and on into my mid-teens. Little seemed to change around there and I think that was OK with him. There was a certain comfort and peace that came from this consistent routine of life in a home where everything and everyone had a place.

My grandfather was a Master Carpenter. To this day I, as well as my parents and many others, have furniture and other pieces of his craftsmanship. He built many boats, houses and anything else that could be made out of wood. For many years of his life he built and made things without the use of any power tools.

For instance, the handheld circular saw was not invented until 1923. In 1924 it was put into production by the founders of SKIL. Today the handheld circular saw is commonly called a Skilsaw. I was talking to my dad and we figured that my grandfather got his first skilsaw around 1950. Up until then he strictly used manual tools. That means for about the first twenty years of his working life he built everything with manual tools! Now imagine the range of emotion, excitement and apprehension he must have experienced with his first electric circular saw.

Knowing him, I suppose he was resistant to the general idea of change. He may even have thought it would be cheating and a total abandonment of true craftsmanship to use an electric saw. However, once he got past the initial point of possible craftsman treason, the thought of less laborious sawing and increased time for design, probably became more appealing.

I suppose we all resist change to some degree. When we have been doing something the same way for a long time, in some cases most of our lives, there is a certain amount of peace, comfort and safety attached to holding on to "the way we've always done it."

By the time I came along, Grandfather had long been proficient with his Skilsaw. When he had a lot of sawing to do he would break that bad boy out and have lumber cut into project sizes in nothing flat! He would still use his hand saw when there was only a piece or two to cut, instead of running an extension cord just to use his circular saw for a few cuts, but he never went back to sawing all his wood by hand.

In a spiritual sense, we can choose God's way to live our lives, or we can decide to live the way we've always done it. We can do life in our own strength, or we can plug into the power of God. In other words, we can saw through this life with just our own "arm strength" or buzz through with the "Skilsaw power" of God and never have to go back to our old ways again!

"For my thoughts are not your thoughts,
neither are your ways my ways,"
declares the Lord.
"As the heavens are higher than the earth,
so are my ways higher than your ways
and my thoughts than your thoughts. (Isaiah 55: 8-9)

GROUP DISCUSSION

1. At whose house, or at what place, did you usually experience comfort and peace when you were there?

2. Do you have a favorite new tool? What? Why is it your favorite? (Mine is my new self-propelled, mulching, lawn-slaying mower! Yeah baby!)

3. What changes might you be resisting because you are comfortable with "the way you've always done it"?

4. Pray that God would show you any area where changes are needed in your life and for Him to show you His will and way to accomplish those changes.

6

Tools And Talents

Some of you will remember land line telephones. That's right, for those of you who came along after cell phones were common, we used to have phones in our houses that had a rotary dial. These phones sat on desks, end tables or were mounted to walls! Barbaric, medieval and totally uncool! We also had phone books, with all the local phone numbers listed.

We always kept a phone book near each phone. Usually, for the desk phones, we just laid the phone book on the end table and put the phone on top of the phone book. The wall mounted phone was usually in a kitchen, where it was a bit more of a challenge to find a convenient place for a phone book.

It was kind of slow one day while I was employed at a sheet metal shop, so I decided to make a phone book holder to mount on the kitchen wall at my mom's house, that way she could have her phone book handy right under her phone. We used to call these personal projects "scrounge jobs." I guess I could have asked the boss if there was some (real) work I could do, but it was slow, so I went ahead with my personal project.

I cut two pieces of nice aluminum (the shop's, I didn't pay for it). I grabbed the tools I needed (again, the shop's, not mine). After cutting, bending and fitting the pieces together I proceeded to drill a few holes where I would install the rivets to hold it together. As I was drilling a hole, a sharp pain shot through my finger and I dropped the metal like a hot rock!

When I first looked at the 1/8th inch hole in my finger (about 1/4 inch deep), it looked like hamburger. Then it started throbbing and bleeding all over the place!

I finished the phone book holder and mounted it on Mom's kitchen wall.

Often times, when we use our tools and talents for the wrong reasons, there will be consequences to pay. When it gets right down to it, I stole some metal, used my (issued for other jobs) tools and talents to give my mom a gift, supposedly from me. Kind of like burning CD's and DVD's you didn't pay for or have a license to copy. Oooh, that one hit some people!

Anyway, God has given us tools and talents to be used for His Kingdom work. There are teachers, preachers, musicians, givers, servers and the list is endless! Yet if we teach the wrong thing, preach the wrong words, praise the wrong gods, keep when we should give, take when we should serve ... you get where I'm going ... we damage the Kingdom, not build it!

... for God's gifts and his call are irrevocable. (Romans 11:29)
Let's use our tools and talents for that which they were issued to us, to build His Kingdom!

More about the gifts He gives us and their proper use is found in 1 Corinthians 12 and 1 Corinthians 14.

GROUP DISCUSSION

1. Have you ever done a scrounge job or in some way used the tools of your workplace for your personal use, without permission? What?

2. If you answered yes to #1, share any unfavorable consequences you faced as a result of your actions.

3. What tools (gifts) and talents has God given you? How have you or how can you use them for building up His Kingdom?

4. Pray that He will show you how and where you might use the gifts He has given you.

7

TAPE MEASURE OF INTEGRITY

In the years past when I worked construction I always kept a tape measure on my belt. The real purpose of a tape measure on a construction site is to be your emergency break time tool. If you need to stop working for a few minutes, you can just pull that bad boy off your belt and act like you're measuring something!

Honestly now, this is only a semi-joke! I've seen and know of guys who do just that. However, the intended and correct use of a tape measure is to take precise measurements so as to build something to its exact specifications. For instance, if the measurements are only slightly off at the ground floor of a ten story building, by the time you get to the top you will have built the Leaning Tower of Pisa, if it's still standing at all!

So let's say you need to be sure the layout for a ground floor is square (meaning the measurements are correct everywhere), you would use a tape measure to check it out. The tape measure doesn't lie. It is the same for whoever uses it. It gives an honest measurement. It is a "fair scale" to check the "value" of the work. You would need to measure all sides to make sure they are exactly the same AND measure corner to corner and other corner to other corner to make sure they are exactly the same. If they are, then you have a square floor.

"Being square" with someone used to be a common saying that meant everything was even between two people or two groups. If I bought something from someone and I paid them the total and fair price for my purchase, then we were "square" or "squared away." We had not tried to con, cheat, beat or swindle one another. He had asked a fair price, I paid what it was worth, and we had completed an honest deal with the utmost integrity.

I believe God wants us to be honest and fair in all our interactions with people including financial transactions, trades, and information exchange. We should proceed honestly and fairly, coming to a price that is fair for a purchase, or things of even value in a swap, and the truth in the exchange of information. Using honest measurements and values (scales) in our dealings with others is the squared away foundation that we can build on to become Godly men of integrity.

The Lord detests dishonest scales,
but accurate weights find favor with him. (Proverbs 11:1)

I know, my God, that you test the heart and are pleased with integrity. (1 Chronicles 29:17)

GROUP DISCUSSION

1. Has anyone ever cheated or lied to you in a transaction?

2. Have you ever justified "getting even" or cheating someone else?

3. Forgiveness is the tool to use to be "squared away" with someone. This includes the giving and receiving of forgiveness. Are you "squared away" with anyone you may have been dishonest with?

4. Are you "squared away" with God?

5. Pray with each other that you can forgive those who have wronged you, as God has forgiven us.

Do not judge, and you will not be judged. Do not condemn,
and you will not be condemned. Forgive, and you will be forgiven.
(Luke 6:37)

8

Remove The Clamps

My grandfather spent a lot of time working on and caring for boats. In fact, he used to build small boats in his back yard to make a few extra bucks. It was quite a skill back in his day to build boats because most boats were made out of wood and the wood had to be "shaped," particularly the bow (front) of the boat.

The bow had to be shaped so the boat could cut smoothly through the water. This meant the wood for the bow of the boat had to be cut with angles and curves and then be shaped or bent to come together at the front of the boat in a "V" shape or rounded somewhat so that the boat would cut through the water nicely.

I've watched with amazement as he formed these pieces of wood into the bow of a boat. He cut curves and angles with precision. Then he would shape them together, installing screws in precise locations and gluing every joint and seam. Finally he would place clamps on the now fastened and glued bow of the boat to hold it all together.

After a period of time there came the moment for removing the clamps. He now had faith that the screws and the glue would hold the boat together, so he removed the clamps. It stayed together every time! The boat was now seaworthy.

Sure it would need some maintenance from time to time, a little scraping here, a little paint there. And sure, maybe a little time in dry dock once in a while to get restored to "like new," so it could go to sea again.

I think we are often like a boat under construction. We have our "clamps on," we are the ones who have control of our lives. We have been wonderfully, masterfully created by God, like my Grandfather forming that boat. Yet we sometimes don't want to take the clamps off and trust that God used enough glue to keep us together in the rough seas of life.

Here's the deal. We are going to have to sail into this sea of our lives and there will be storms, fog and navigation problems. And our ship will not stay afloat with the clamps of our control fastened tightly to us.

We will have to take off the clamps (give God control of our lives) to be able to cut through the storms, see in the fog and ultimately arrive at our destination, the calm seas of Heaven.

We are fearfully and wonderfully made. He didn't "build" us so precisely and carefully just for us to set sail and sink. He made us to complete a voyage that ultimately has us docking at His home port!

> *For you created my inmost being;*
> *you knit me together in my mother's womb.*
> *I praise you because I am fearfully and wonderfully made;*
> *your works are wonderful,*
> *I know that full well.*
> *My frame was not hidden from you*
> *when I was made in the secret place,*
> *when I was woven together in the depths of the earth.*
> *Your eyes saw my unformed body;*
> *all the days ordained for me were written in your book*
> *before one of them came to be.* (Psalm 139:13-16)

GROUP DISCUSSION

1. What is the coolest thing you ever built?

2. In what areas of your life have you removed your clamps (given God total control)?

3. In what areas have you *not* removed your clamps?

4. Pray for each other that God would help you remove your clamps and give Him control, trusting Him in every area of your life.

9

The Brake Tool

I had to have some brake work done on my old truck the other day. It reminded me of the first time I tried to do some brake work on my first car. The first few times I worked on my own car were less than complete successes. I did not have the right tools, talent or knowledge to take on these mechanical endeavors.

My first experience in major car repair (outside of changing a fuse) was a complete engine rebuild. I was sixteen years old and my car had a lifter knocking. This was not viewed as an awesome sounding engine by me or my hot rod friends. I decided to tear the entire engine down and re-build it. I knew nothing of the process or the tools required, and I lacked the talent to properly complete the job. I did however proceed, figuring I would learn as I go. I blew the engine a few days after completing the job!

Days prior to my engine rebuild, I had to repair the brakes on the same car. This experience should have been a red flag to me that I was not yet a certified shade tree mechanic capable of an engine rebuild!

I popped off the hubcap, removed the wheel and hub, exposing the brakes on the left front wheel. This car had the old drum brakes with that extremely tight spring on the brake that had to be removed to work on the brakes. There was a special tool that was made to remove the spring by stretching it out while maintaining a good grip. I didn't own one, and besides, I had a pair of pliers. I decided I would just manhandle that spring off of the brake!

I couldn't get it off for anything. I got my dad to give it a try. He came out, put a death grip on that spring and yanked! I honestly don't remember if he got the spring off, but those pliers cracked him right in the forehead! Although it was bleeding like mad, it was a clean cut not requiring stitches at the emergency room. They just put a couple of pieces of that (new at the time) stitch tape on the gash and sent us home.

God gives us tools and talents. We are told many times in the Proverbs to go after wisdom and knowledge. In the two examples above I did not have the tools or the knowledge to do the job right, so it wouldn't matter much if I had the yet undiscovered talent. God gave us gifts, tools, talents and knowledge to carry out service in the Kingdom according to His will. When we do not use God's gifts, tools, talents and knowledge correctly or use them for the wrong reasons, things can go awry and the consequences could be seriously negative!

If we are musically talented, use that gift in praising Him. If we speak well, tell about Him. If we are teachers, teach others about Him. If we can earn money, give. We should use what He has given us to give back to His Kingdom.

> *Now may the God of peace, who through the blood of the eternal covenant brought back from the dead our Lord Jesus, that great Shepherd of the sheep, equip you with everything good for doing his will, and may he work in us what is pleasing to him, through Jesus Christ, to whom be glory for ever and ever. Amen.* (Hebrews 13:20-21)

GROUP DISCUSSION

1. Have you ever tried to tackle a job that you've never done before, with no knowledge of how to proceed? How did that work out for you?

2. Have you ever (prior to taking on a task for the first time) sought out the wisdom, knowledge and direction of an individual skilled in that task, to guide you and help you through that process? Did that turn out better for you than the answer to Question 1?

3. Based on either or both of your answers to the first two questions, would it seem a wise idea to seek out God's guidance in your life decisions through His Word, prayer and Godly counsel?

4. Do you have a testimony of how a situation in your life worked out for you when you sought out God's will and leading vs a time you did not seek Him and proceeded to try to resolve a tough situation by your own devices?

5. Are you in a situation right now that you need God to guide you and move on your behalf? Share this with your group and pray for one another.

10

Love Is The Paint

My grandfather was, and my dad and oldest son are, excellent carpenters and woodworkers. I may be missing a few of the "craftsman genes" (probably patience and one or two intricate skill genes), but I get by.

I have been using some of my free time lately to work on our deck here at the house. I reinforced the original deck, built and attached a new ramp to it and continued sprucing it up little by little. However, the difference in my skills and the three men mentioned above is obvious.

If any of those three would have completed a deck themselves, the only need for paint or stain would be to add color to a beautiful piece of work. In my case, paint needs to be applied to cover my multitude of repairs to misplaced screw holes, hammer dents in the wood next to nails I missed and all the other boo boos of this amateur carpenter.

It's not unlike my personal life. I am far from the best carpenter in the family and I am very far from the best Christian in God's family. I'm only in God's family because of my belief and trust in Jesus and what He did for me, not my own remarkable abilities to be Godly. So how do the marks (sin I commit and the hurts I cause) get covered up? Love is the paint in the Kingdom.

Jesus' act of love covers (paints over) my sin. My love for others can paint over hurt I inflict on them. If I have an argument with Hannah Pooh (we occasionally do, believe it or not), acts of love by me such as asking for her forgiveness, soft, kind, heartfelt words and maybe throwing in a dinner date can paint over my sin or hurt I inflicted on her.

If we have sin in our lives, Jesus has an endless supply of Love (paint) to apply to us if we just ask. If we have hurt someone, we too have love to spread around to the careless damage we have inflicted on others. It works! Try it, I dare you!

Above all, love each other deeply, because love covers over a multitude of sins. (1 Peter 4:8)

GROUP DISCUSSION

1. What fixer-upper skills do you have (or lack)? This is for fun, so tell the truth!

2. Have you allowed Jesus to cover (paint over) your sin?

3. As believers, we have the love of God in us! Is there any sin or hurt you have inflicted on someone that could use a little painting over?

4. Thank God in your prayers for the Love and forgiveness He has poured out (painted) on us. Ask Him to show you if there is anyone who you may need to love and ask forgiveness from, to heal any hurt or sin.

11

RUSTY PLIERS

Over the years, after completing a task, I have occasionally forgotten to put all my tools back in my toolbox. I have left a hammer outside and it was rained on, dropped needle-nose pliers in the yard and not found them for days and left side-cutters outside on the opposite side of a large job site, exposed to the elements. Later I have found them rusted and unusable.

Tools are expensive and I want to take good care of them. They are important to my task and they need to be in good working order so that I may do my job or project well and successfully. When I find a tool in poor condition I do what I have to do to restore it to being a good, functional tool.

For instance, when I have found a pair of pliers that I have left outside days before, it is likely to be rusted to the point of being locked up and of no use. I will get a wire cloth to brush the rust off and put oil on the pliers to loosen the joint so that it is clean and functional again. Some types of pliers have a small nut and screw that may need to be replaced with a new part to make it work again.

I think there are similarities here to how God views us. However, unlike the tools, we often have the choice in the matter of being exposed to the "elements" of this world. Other times we are faced with difficulties through no fault or choice of our own. In either case, we can find ourselves exposed to terrible "weather."

Like my tools, but to a much greater degree, God cares for us. He loves us, is concerned for us and does not want us rusted, stuck, and of no use for His purposes. We are expensive to Him, costing Him the life of His Son. We are important to Him for His Kingdom's work. He desires for us to be "functional tools" at work in His will and for His glory.

Yet in our case, as opposed to my tools, when we are hindered by the elements of this world, we have to choose to be restored by Him to "good as new" condition. When we call out to Him, He will come pick us up, clean us, put His oil upon us and even give us a new (part) heart, restoring us to Him and His purposes.

> *I will sprinkle clean water on you, and you will be clean; I will cleanse you from all your impurities and from all your idols. I will give you a new heart and put a new spirit in you; I will remove from you your heart of stone and give you a heart of flesh.* (Ezekiel 36:25-26)

> *Is anyone among you sick? Let them call the elders of the church to pray over them and anoint them with oil in the name of the Lord. And the prayer offered in faith will make the sick person well; the Lord will raise them up. If they have sinned, they will be forgiven.* (James 5:14-15)

GROUP DISCUSSION

1. Have you ever left one of your tools out in the weather only to find it later in an unusable condition? Explain.

2. Has God ever restored you from a time that you became "rusted and unusable"? How?

3. Are you exposing yourself to any elements of this world that may be hinder your effectiveness as a tool in the hands of the God? If so, identify those elements.

4. Pray together, for one another, that God will restore any areas of your life that have become rusted by pouring His oil of restoration on your life. He is faithful! He will do it!

12

SHOCKING!

My grandfather was a carpenter all of his working life. For a good bit of his early working years he used hand tools, no power tools. As time went on, more and more power tools became available. A necessary tool to make power tools portable and available to the carpenter at any job location was the extension cord.

I remember grabbing an extension cord at a job site once after it had rained. I had not unplugged the cord before beginning to roll it up. Shocking! The power continues to flow through an extension cord as long as it is plugged into the power source.

I liken our lives as believers to being extension cords in the Kingdom. If we are plugged in to God as our power source, we can do great things! We can have victory in every way, overcoming hardship, sin, and persecution. We can witness and be used by the Father to draw others to Jesus. We can teach others how to follow Christ according to His Word. There will be power in our prayers as we seek to do His will that He makes known to us. He will use us to further His Kingdom!

Do you want some of that?! The way to get this power flowing through us is to plug into the power of God. Here's the catch: Unlike a common, lifeless extension cord, if we want His power flowing through us, we have to choose to plug into His power, and it is High Voltage! You will be shocked by His power! So in plugging in to His power we need to be guided by His will, so as to not suffer a power outage.

Here's a couple of places in the Bible that speak to the power of God:

I tell you the truth, anyone who has faith in me will do what I have been doing. He will do even greater things than these, because I am going to the Father. (John 14:12)

I can do all things through Christ who strengthens me.
(Philippians 4:13)

Plug into that!

GROUP DISCUSSION

1. Have you ever received an electrical shock? How did it happen?

2. Share a situation in your life that, had you been plugged into the power of God, it may have turned out better.

3. Share a time when the power of God was flowing in your life and God gave you the victory.

4. What might you seek the power of God for in your life right now?

5. Pray for God to move mightily in one another's lives.

13

Put The Gloves On ... Every Time

Working in a lumber yard can lead to all kinds of scrapes, bruises and injuries. While I worked in a lumber yard, I used all kinds of safety measures to try to prevent injury to myself and others. This included staying clear of moving machinery such as forklifts carrying stacks of lumber, wearing a hard hat and lifting properly.

The most common injury was splinters in my hands. To prevent this I kept a good pair of gloves in my tool box. Upon my arrival at work, my gloves went straight into my back pocket where they would be handy at any time. It was a wise and effective way to keep my hands from being stuck with splinters and scraped against racks where the wood was stacked.

Sometimes I would forget to put on my gloves before grabbing some lumber with my hands and I would scrape my hands on the metal racks, peeling some skin off. Other times I would just choose not to put my gloves on because I was only going to grab a piece or two of lumber for a customer. It so often happened that when I chose this shortcut, I would inevitably run a nice size splinter into my hand!

One of the things our God offers us is protection. To receive His protection we must be willing to put on the "gloves" He offers us. Life on this earth is often like a lumber yard full of hazards that can potentially cause us (or even others) harm if we do not follow His safety guidelines.

We may think that we can handle situations in our own strength and quickly, without seeking His will, we decide to just snatch a couple of boards off of our stack of concerns. This could result in our being injured or cause injury to someone else, due to our carelessness in not seeking God's will. In many situations in life, things may look neatly stacked and easy to get to, but the load can shift unexpectedly and our situation can become much worse.

When we need to move some lumber in life, let's be sure to put on our spiritual gloves by seeking God's guidance through His Word, prayer and Godly advice from those who have worked in His lumber yard longer than us. In this way we can not only be successful in getting the "wood" we need but also getting it down safely without causing unnecessary injury to anyone.

> *But the Lord is faithful, and he will strengthen you and protect you from the evil one.* (2 Thessalonians 3:3)

> *Finally, be strong in the Lord and in his mighty power. Put on the full armor of God, so that you can take your stand against the devil's schemes. For our struggle is not against flesh and blood, but against the rulers, against the authorities, against the powers of this dark world and against the spiritual forces of evil in the heavenly realms. Therefore put on the full armor of God, so that when the day of evil comes, you may be able to stand your ground, and after you have done everything, to stand. Stand firm then, with the belt of truth buckled around your waist, with the breastplate of righteousness in place, and with your feet fitted with the readiness that comes from the gospel of peace. In addition to all this, take up the shield of faith, with which you can extinguish all the flaming arrows of the evil one. Take the helmet of salvation and the sword of the Spirit, which is the word of God.* (Ephesians 6:10-17)

GROUP DISCUSSION

1. Have you ever been injured when you chose not to follow safety instructions and procedures?

2. Name some splinters you have received when you chose not to follow God's "safety instructions."

3. How might you, in the future, put on God's safety gear when faced with a "stack of wood" to move?

4. Pray together that God would show you His will and way for you to safely move the next stack of wood that life or the enemy puts in your path.

14

The Door

I remember as a small boy watching my grandfather install doors. Back then doors didn't come pre-hung in a door jamb. For all practical purposes, the door he was going to install came over-sized and had to be cut, trimmed, have hardware installed and then be fitted into the door opening by him, the carpenter.

Exterior doors were solid wood. He would begin by measuring the opening and then sawing the door to the size of the opening. He would then use a wood chisel to cut the slots in the edge of the door and the door jamb, where the hinges would be installed. Next he would place the door in the jamb and mark it precisely where it needed trimming to fit exactly in the doorway. He would often use a hand plane to trim the door down to fit properly and close precisely. This step was followed by using sandpaper to smooth all the edges. Lastly, the hinges were installed and adjusted so that the door would swing level.

This was a meticulous process requiring patience and craftsmanship. I have hung doors that are already pre-hung in a door jamb and it is no easy task to do properly, but my grandfather knew what it required to make the door work right and serve its purpose.

(I know that if I don't clarify myself here before some read the rest of this story, they will say: "The Word says Jesus is the door." And that is absolutely correct! He is the way, the truth and the life, no one comes to the Father but by Him! He is the door to salvation, the Father and Heaven. Yet for most of us, weren't we introduced to Jesus by someone who opened up their lives in Him to us? That's the door we can be to others.)

We as believers are called to show others the way to Jesus. But if we are going to be a door, we need to be "fitted" to the doorway we are going be opening. We don't come pre-hung, fitted and ready to be a "doorway." God works in our lives to shape us into the door we need to be for others to see Jesus in us.

At some points in our lives we can be as hard as petrified wood. Yet Jesus can work in us to saw away sin, such as pride and disobedience.

He will chisel away at our hard hearts and install His Holy Spirit in us so that we are connected to Him. He will plane our fleshly edges so that we don't get stuck as we serve Him. He will sand our edges so that we speak the truth in love. He will make the adjustments to us so that we can open easily, serving His purpose.

The difference between us and the wood doors my grandfather installed is that we can choose to be stuck in the doorway. We can refuse to be shaped into the most effective door for His purposes. We can absolutely lock ourselves up and be of no use in being a door for God to draw the lost into His presence.

Sure, the lost can find another door, but if we're not a doorway, then we're a wall! Let's allow the Carpenter to shape us into a door He can open easily for souls to come through to Him!

GROUP DISCUSSION

1. Tell about a task you completed that was meticulous and time consuming, requiring patience and skillful perseverance.

2. How has God been shaping you to fit your doorway (calling)? Where has He made the big cuts, chipped away and smoothed your edges?

3. How are you doing as a door in the doorway for others to get to Jesus?

4. Pray that God will always adjust you where and when needed to be a door that opens for others to meet Jesus.

15

Follow Your Blueprints

As a young man I worked quite a bit in construction. My dad was a Construction Superintendent, the boss on site over the entire project. I worked for him some and on other building projects as well, but always at large construction sites such as schools, hospitals, high rises and the like.

I sometimes did some iron work or general labor, but for the most part I did carpentry work. Most of the carpentry I was doing had to do with building forms for concrete pours, and some layout for and installation of things like doors, windows, cabinets and miscellaneous other tasks. I did not do plumbing, electrical, A/C, heating and other jobs that required talents other than what I possessed.

The superintendent had the blueprints (detailed drawings) for the entire project. His blueprints showed the "big picture," specifically how to complete the entire building. There were also blueprints (plans) specific to each crafts job on the site. For instance, there were electrical prints showing where and how to run and hook up the wiring; plumbing prints to show where to run pipe and hook up water lines and prints showing where to run A/C ducts, etc. Although he would have a complete set of the blueprints, the boss would only give me prints that showed me where and how to do my task. I didn't need to know what, how or why the electricians, plumbers and A/C guys were going to do their job.

Essentially, the boss had the big picture view of things and how they were to progress. He had to work out who would do what, when, where, how, and why so that the job could be completed correctly and on time. So the boss gave out tasks to each craft based on his knowledge of the big picture. I, nor the other crafts, needed to know the "why" of every task, we only needed the page of the blueprints that showed us what to do next.

Had I meddled in the other crafts' work or been so concerned about the how, when, where, and why of their tasks, the building could have been completed late or even incorrectly constructed. This would result in the building not being as useful as originally intended.

As believers we are to help in building others up in the Kingdom. I know myself, that I have often wondered: "Why God? Why me? Why now? Why this way? What about so and so doing this task? That's not an important job, God! Give that one to someone else, put me out front! What is this going to accomplish? Where is this going? What's going to be the result here? I don't think that guy is doing what he's supposed to do, I'll fix it!"

When my attitude is like that of someone not wanting to follow God's blueprint because I can't see the big picture, then I'm hindering the building up of someone in the Kingdom. I could quit the job, or maybe get fired from that project and replaced by someone who will follow the blueprint the Boss gives him, trusting that He sees the big picture. Or I could just build according to the blueprints He gives me.

> For I know the plans I have for you," declares the Lord, "plans to prosper you and not to harm you, plans to give you hope and a future. (Jeremiah 29:11)

GROUP DISCUSSION

1. When have you not known the big picture of some task that you were assigned and it frustrated you?

2. Have you ever wondered: "Why me, God?" or "Wouldn't it be better if I did it this way?" Explain.

3. When you question God, is it in order to decide if you're going to obey Him? One of the ways we show our love for God is in obeying Him.

4. Ask God to guide you and to give you the faith to obey the Blueprints He gives you.

16

BUILD ON THE RIGHT FOUNDATION

In my young adult years as a construction worker there were many hard, laborious jobs to be accomplished. Certainly there were enough without making mistakes that would cause extra work. Yet assumptions, oversights and hurry contributed to mistakes being made with consequences that require difficult correction.

Concrete is the foundation for most building construction today. I remember on a few occasions the concrete was poured in the wrong place or at the wrong height. We always tested the density of the concrete too. If it did not meet specifications, it should not be poured. If it was poured lacking the correct density, in the wrong place or at the wrong height, then it had to be busted up and removed.

Yeah baby! There's nothing like being on the handle of a 90lb jackhammer for days on end, busting up concrete, putting it in wheelbarrows, and pushing that load off site to be hauled off. All it takes is an inch or two off here or there and it has to go. You can't adjust everything in a multi-story building to a misplaced foundation.

Having the foundation right is the only way the building will stand the test of time. Having our foundation right is the only way we will stand in the tests of our lives. In this life we will face storms of a physical, mental, emotional, financial and spiritual nature. Some of these storms will cause damage to our lives (our building). Yet if our foundation is Jesus, we will come through the storms of this life and with His help, we can make repairs to our "building" and emerge from these storms eternally unscathed!

If our foundation is our own strength, money, character, or anything or anyone else but Jesus, we could be blown away at any moment. This is a foundation that needs to be busted up! If we are willing and ask, He will bust up the "concrete" of our faulty misplaced foundation and will help and guide us into building our lives upon Him. He is a perfect foundation from which we will never be blown off and destroyed!

"But the one who hears my words and does not put them into practice is like a man who built a house on the ground without a foundation. The moment the torrent struck that house, it collapsed and its destruction was complete." (Luke 6:49)

GROUP DISCUSSION

1. Have you ever noticed how a storm will sometimes destroy and blow an entire house away, but that the "strong foundation" remains and the house can be rebuilt upon it?

2. Have you ever seen or had to rebuild, repair, or renovate a building damaged by a storm, such as a hurricane or tornado?

3. Did you ever rebuild or repair a relationship after a storm in your life?

4. In the storms of this life is Jesus truly your foundation?

5. Pray with one another that when the storms of life come, you would make Jesus your foundation, no matter the intensity of the storm.

17

CONSUMERS AND THE CONSUMED

In the "natural," a consumer is a person who buys some product and uses that product as he sees fit. The product, a tool for example, is designed for a specific purpose. You drive a nail with a hammer not a putty knife. You cut a board with a saw not a piece of sandpaper. However, many of us have used a knife blade for a screwdriver or a wrench to drive a nail just because the wrong tool was handy. Some correct uses for products we consume might be: a house for shelter, a car for transportation, food to eat, clothes to wear, electricity for power, water to drink...etc.

There are all sorts of advertising and marketing sources we can use to help us decide what products to consume. Magazine articles rate products. There are sale papers, catalogs, and the Internet to see the choices and prices as well as TV and radio ads to entice us to purchase all kinds of goodies.

We consume in the Natural out of need or desire. It is the consumer's choice not the product's decision. But in the Spirit Realm it is God or Satan who will be the consumer and you and I are the products that will be "consumed." The difference is, in the Spiritual, the product has the choice of who will be the consumer and how we will be used by that consumer. The advertising and marketing efforts in the spiritual world for the services of the products are more intense than any sales meeting on earth.

God provides us sources to guide us into making the right choices. These choices are no less than life and death. When we read and study His word, pray and follow the leading of the Holy Spirit, we can make the right choices in obedience and be used for what we were designed. We can do all things through Christ who strengthens us (Philippians 4:13) and if we show our love for God through our obedience we can be in His presence (John 14).

The enemy on the other hand will use any means possible to consume us to the point of being used up for his evil purposes. Temptations that seem to be used by the devil on men include: work, sexual temptations, things that *have* to get done, TV, busyness...etc. Satan comes to steal, kill, and destroy. These are not just strong words, it is his literal game plan.

Every product is created and designed for a specific task, but no matter how perfectly designed, it can still be used for the wrong purposes. This would obviously result in an outcome less than it was created to achieve. We were created and designed to have a personal relationship with Jesus Christ, that would be the perfect use of our design. Remember, before a product can be used it must be bought and paid for, and we have been bought with the highest price. We were purchased by God and the price was His Son.

Choose to be "consumed" by God! Do the things you were designed to carry out for the Kingdom. See God move as you are yielded and "Holy Consumed" by Him.

GROUP DISCUSSION

1. How do you decide what to consume (use or buy)? How much of your decision to consume something is based on need, desire, or whose Kingdom it will benefit?

2. Describe a way you have been consumed by God. Describe a way you have been tempted by Satan.

3. Explain how your talents can be used for God's purposes. Explain how your talents can be wrongfully used for Satan.

4. Ask God to guide you daily, so you will make Godly choices that will make you an effective tool in the hands of the Master Carpenter.

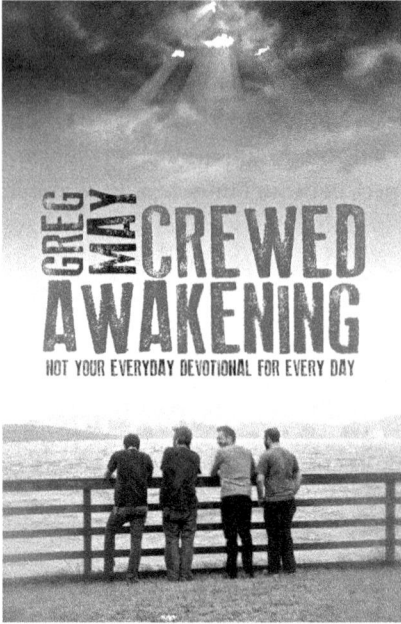

Starting your day with Holy Scripture, bold coffee, and *Crewed Awakening* will jolt you awake to a new life in Christ.

Dr. Geoffrey Lentz
Pastor
First United Methodist
Church
Port St. Joe, FL

What a charming, de-lightful and fresh read!

Renee Crosby
author of *Soup Kitchen for the Soul*

It's in the Bag
Kimberly Gordon

www.ingramcontent.com/pod-product-compliance
Lightning Source LLC
Chambersburg PA
CBHW030309030426
42337CB00012B/654